God has Spoken

Listen & Obey

Carmen R Dulaney

Published by
Columbus Book Publishers
www.columbusbookpublishers.com

Printed in the United States of America

Dedication

To the faithful remnant—those who continue to proclaim the Gospel of the Kingdom regardless of the cost.

To every soul who hungers for truth, longs for righteousness and justice, and dares to obey God's voice.

This book is for those who refuse to compromise in a world full of competing voices.

May you arise, shine, and finish your race in victory.

Acknowledgment

First and foremost, I give glory to God our Father and the Lord Jesus Christ—who called, equipped, and sustained me through the writing of this book. Without Your voice, wisdom, and presence, this work would not exist.

To my family: thank you for your unwavering love, prayers, and belief in this calling. Your support helped strengthen my resolve to obey God's command to speak what He said.

To the Body of Christ, especially those serving in humble places and proclaiming truth with boldness: your labor is not in vain. You are the light in the darkness, the watchmen on the wall, and the hands and feet of Jesus on Earth.

To all who have prayed, encouraged, and challenged me to stay the course—thank you. Every word, conversation, and affirmation made this journey possible.

To all my spiritual leaders who spoke into my life, ordained me as an elder and pastor in God's church, and continue to use me as a prophetic voice, adviser, counselor, pastor, intercessor, and teacher.

And finally, to every reader drawn to these pages: may your heart be awakened, your faith stirred, and your life anchored in God's Word. He has spoken. May we listen—and live accordingly.

About the Author

Carmen is a devoted wife, mother, and grandmother, blessed with a dynamic and Christ-centered family. With a deep desire to honor and please the Lord in all things, she and her husband Keith faithfully partner together to build their marriage and family network on the firm foundation of Jesus Christ, their Rock and Redeemer.

Carmen is a prophetic voice and devoted disciple of Jesus Christ, called to awaken the Church to its true identity and Kingdom assignment. Deeply rooted in Scripture and led by the Holy Spirit, she speaks and writes with boldness, clarity, and compassion—challenging believers to embrace truth, live righteously, and embody God's love in a world desperate for light.

As a spiritual watchman, Carmen carries a burden to confront deception and complacency in the Body of Christ. Her ministry blends biblical insight with modern relevance, calling the Church to repentance, justice, and alignment with God's Word. Through teaching, writing, and exhortation, she equips Christians to fulfill the dominion mandate, stand firm in faith, and proclaim the Gospel with conviction and power.

Carmen's work reflects a deep love for Christ-centered theology, prophetic insight, and transformative discipleship. She passionately addresses issues of injustice, spiritual identity, and Kingdom stewardship—always pointing readers back to Scripture and the heart of God. Her personal testimony and obedience to God's calling have birthed a unique writing voice that combines urgency with grace, conviction with tenderness.

Above all, Carmen desires to see the Bride of Christ prepared for the return of her King—walking in holiness, guided by truth, and filled with the Spirit. Her life and calling are grounded in one enduring message: *God has spoken. Will His people listen, obey, and arise?*

Table of Contents

Introduction

This book flows from a humble and burdened heart—one longing for God's Church to reflect His Kingdom in purity, power, and obedience. As ambassadors of the Lord Jesus Christ, we are called to stand as radiant witnesses of truth and love. Yet much of what the world has witnessed—particularly from American Christianity—reveals a disheartening contradiction: believers tolerating and empowering deception, lawlessness, injustice, immorality, racism, political idolatry, and corruption. These traits speak not of the Spirit's fruit, but of compromise. They expose a grievous reality: many are Christian in name only (C.I.N.O.).

Though a faithful remnant continues to heed the Lord's commands, the entire Church is touched by this spiritual erosion. We must all take responsibility to return to the Lord—not in theory, but in repentance and renewed obedience. Consider the conduct of many professing believers across the past five presidential elections, during the 2020 pandemic crisis, and in the slow descent into spiritual apathy we now witness. The light of God's righteousness and justice has grown dim in our nation.

This is not to ignore the rebellion among unbelievers, who also stand accountable before God. Romans 1:18–23 makes it clear: those who suppress the truth in unrighteousness are without excuse. God's invisible attributes—His eternal power and divine nature—have been revealed since creation. They knew Him but did not glorify Him, choosing instead to exchange His glory for idols. And still, the greater tragedy is when God's people abandon the truth they claim to know.

This is no time for the Church to be silent, fearful, distracted, or powerless. We are called to proclaim the Gospel—not just in words, but in righteous action. Though none of us has fulfilled this perfectly, the time has come for the Bride of Christ to rise with holy zeal, preparing for His return through obedient and consecrated living.

Just as Nineveh turned from its wickedness at the preaching of Jonah, we too must respond before judgment falls. We must heed the wisdom of King Solomon, who sought forgiveness for Israel when they turned from disobedience: "If My people who are called by My name will humble themselves, and pray and seek My face, and turn from their wicked ways, then I will hear from heaven and will forgive their sin and heal their land" (2 Chronicles 7:14).

The time is now—because the moral condition of a nation is inseparable from the integrity of its spiritual leaders. All will give account to God, who judges the nations with righteousness (Matthew 25:31–46; Psalm 110:6). May this book stir the Church to repent, awaken, and shine once more with the light of Christ.

Chapter 1: Hearing God's Voice

Those final three words rang in my spirit like a divine alarm. *Listen to Him!* This was not a suggestion; it was a command. It grieved me deeply as I considered the spiritual lethargy among Believers today—so many drifting from Gospel proclamation, sound doctrine, and wholehearted discipleship.

A Divine Encounter

Toward the end of 2023, in a quiet moment with the Lord, three words emerged clearly: **God has spoken!** Then came the charge: **"Tell them what I said."** That divine instruction stirred a holy urgency. His voice within me was loud and unmistakable—piercing through every distraction. And I knew: His message was meant not just for me, but for His people.

Living According to His Word

God has already told us how to live in the world He created for us (Psalm 24:1, 115:16). But we don't always listen. As I pondered His command, the responsibility felt massive. How do we relay His message faithfully when the world is loud with competing voices?

We do so, first and foremost, by a personal commitment to faithfully obey all of God's Word by reading, studying, and obeying it. This leads to the ability to discern God's voice amidst the clamor, and communicate His message with integrity, truth, and authenticity.

Abraham's Response to God's Voice

The call reminded me of Abraham. In Genesis 12:1, God called him to leave everything familiar and go to a land God would later reveal. Abraham obeyed *because he heard.* When God speaks, human reasoning steps aside. It's no longer about logic—it's about obedience.

Listen to His Son

God then led me to Matthew 17:5:

"This is My beloved Son, with whom I am well-pleased; listen to Him."

Those final words—*Listen to Him*—captivated me. They reawakened my awareness of how often we, the Church, neglect our mission. We fail to proclaim the Gospel, make disciples, and teach sound doctrine. I knew then that I must speak boldly, even if the message is uncomfortable.

Discerning the True Voice

The airwaves are filled with "prophetic" voices that do not echo heaven. Like the Bereans (Acts 17:10–12), we must examine Scripture to confirm what we hear. My own prayers often cry for truth to rise above deception in our land. As Paul writes in 1 Timothy 3:15, the Church is the *pillar and ground of the truth*. Not *a* truth, but *the* truth.

A Watchman's Call

One day, in quiet communion with the Lord, He spoke again: **"I called you to be a watchman."** I was stunned. This wasn't a title I claimed—it was a calling I received. I've read about prophets who were called watchmen in the Bible, but it was not on my spiritual radar as an assignment. I immediately searched the Scriptures for intel. The prophet Ezekiel was called to be a watchman for the nation of Israel. We can read about this in Ezekiel 3:17, 4-10 (NASB):

"Son of man, I have appointed you a watchman to the house of Israel; whenever you hear a word from My mouth, warn them from Me. 4 Then He said to me, 'Son of Man, go to the house of Israel and speak with My words to them. 5 For you are not being sent to a people of unintelligible speech or difficult language, but to the house of Israel, 6 nor to many peoples of unintelligible speech or difficult language,

whose words you cannot understand. But I have sent you to them who should listen to you; [7] yet the house of Israel will not be willing to listen to you, since they are not willing to listen to Me. Surely, the whole house of Israel is stubborn and obstinate. [8] Behold, I have made your face as hard as their faces and your forehead as hard as their foreheads. [9] Like emery harder than flint, I have made your forehead. Do not be afraid of them or be dismayed before them, though they are a rebellious house.' [10] Moreover, He said to me, "Son of man, take into your heart all My words which I will speak to you and listen closely. [11] Go to the exiles, to the sons of your people, and speak to them and tell them, whether they listen or not, "Thus says the Lord God."

The Lord made it clear: speak His word, whether the people listen or not. Resistance doesn't revoke the message. Our role is to warn, to call forth, and to proclaim—without fear.

Heeding His Word

The Hebrew word for heed is *shamar* and means to *watch, guard, and keep.* Webster defines it as giving careful attention, consideration, or to mind. Our lives reflect what we give attention to—whether God's Word or the world's wisdom. When I've wandered, I've learned to **STOP, DROP,**

AND ROLL:

Stop and acknowledge where I strayed

Drop into honest repentance

Roll forward by prayer and obedience

Let's empty ourselves of anything contrary to God's Word. Let's incline our ears to His voice.

As Believers, the mental, emotional, and spiritual state of our lives is a reflection of who and what consumes our time, focus, trust, and devotion.

Rhema & Logos

God's Word is expressed both as **Rhema** (a specific, spoken word from God, frequently an insight from the Holy Spirit. The other is **Logos** (the written, totality of the Word of God—Jesus, the Living Word) John 1:1. Pastor Jack Hayford explains Logos beautifully:

"Jesus is the living Logos (John 1:1), the Bible is the written Logos (Hebrews 4:12), and the Holy Spirit utters the spoken Logos (1 Corinthians 2:13)."

The significance of Rhema (distinct from *Logos*) is illustrated in Ephesians 6:17, where the reference is not to the Scriptures as a whole but to that portion which the

Believer wields as a sword in a time of need. *"Take the helmet of salvation and the sword of the Spirit, which is the rhema of God."* When Rhema flows from Logos, we wield it like a sword—timely, precise, and powerful. A prerequisite is the regular storing of the mind with Scripture. Rhema is the revelation of the Logos. Rhema reveals the Logos to address specific challenges and assignments. We need both to walk fully in faith.

Final Thoughts

God speaks because He loves. His voice corrects, equips, and restores. And He calls each of us to steward His Word with reverence and boldness. As you read, may your heart awaken to His command: **"Listen to Him."** There is no greater pursuit than obeying the voice of God and proclaiming His truth in a world desperate for direction.

Prayer

Lord, help us to hear your voice with attention, embrace your Word, and respond with obedience and joy. May we receive boldness to declare what You have spoken no matter the consequences. Make us over in heart, in order that our lives may indeed reflect You. Teach us to hear and heed Your commands like faithful ones, watchmen, and ambassadors of Jesus Christ. Empty us of all that contradicts Your truth, and align our will to Yours. Grant us the discernment to hear Your voice amidst many voices, so that we may walk in Your ways and be a light in the darkness. Equip us to encourage one another to stand firm on the whole counsel of Your Word, and may our words and deeds bring honor to Your name. Grant us grace to live as obedient children and faithful stewards, rendering the Gospel of Your Kingdom with all our being. In Jesus' mighty name, we pray. Amen.

Reflective Questions

1. What specific word or instruction has God spoken to you recently?

   _____

   _____

   _____

   _____

2. In what areas of your life are you being called to "heed" or listen more closely to God?

   _____

   _____

   _____

   _____

3. How can you ensure your daily witness reflects the life of Christ more fully?

   _____

   _____

   _____

   _____

4. Where might you need to "stop, drop, and roll" back into

obedience this week?

_____

_____

_____

_____

Chapter 2
A Huge Problem

There is a growing problem in the Body of Christ—one that grieves the heart of God. We often fail to listen to, heed, and obey His Holy Word, especially when it challenges our personal plans or confronts our agendas. The Bible is not merely a book of inspiration; it is the constitution of God's Kingdom. It contains His commands, statutes, ordinances, laws, principles, and prophecies for every generation.

From Genesis to Revelation, God calls humanity to obedience. From the first command—*"Thou shalt not…"*—to the final warning—*"If anyone takes away from the words of the book of this prophecy…"*—we are reminded that disobedience carries eternal consequences.

"Let us hear the conclusion of the whole matter: Fear God and keep His commandments, For this is man's all. For God will bring every work into judgment, including every secret thing, Whether good or evil." —Ecclesiastes 12:13–14

Disobedience fractures fellowship, but obedience brings alignment with God's will and protection under His covering.

The High Stakes of Disobedience

Can you imagine standing before the throne of God and not hearing the words:

"Well done, good and faithful servant"?

Adam and Eve forfeited eternal fellowship with God through one act of disobedience. We must not assume we are immune simply because we attend church, pray, or give. These are good and expected—but what about loving our enemies? What about hidden prejudices, political biases, or selective morality?

Let's ask ourselves:

Do we apply Scripture equally to all people?

Do we condemn homosexuality but ignore adultery and fornication—sins that equally separate us from God?

"Do you not know that the unrighteous will not inherit the Kingdom of God? Do not be deceived. Neither fornicators, nor idolaters, nor adulterers, nor homosexuals, nor sodomites, nor thieves, nor covetous, nor drunkards, nor revilers, nor extortioners will inherit the Kingdom of God. [11] *And such were some of you. But you were washed, but you were sanctified, but you were justified in the name of the Lord Jesus and by the Spirit of our God." (1 Corinthians 6:9-*

11)

This passage reminds us that all sin separates, but Christ restores.

"And such were some of you. But you were washed…sanctified…justified in the name of the Lord Jesus."

We are not called to condemn—we are called to invite. We must desire salvation and abundant life for all people, just as Christ does.

A Cry for the Church

The cry of my heart is for the Lord's Church to return to our Father's business: advancing His Kingdom through Jesus Christ. Hypocrisy and corruption must no longer define us. We cannot afford to be casual about our calling.

He alone is the way, the truth, and the life (John 14:6). Let us not replace Him with worldly solutions, self indulgences, or political ideologies. Let us return to the simplicity and power of the Gospel.

A Dwelling Place for His Spirit

If you feel a heaviness reading this, that may be the Holy Spirit stirring you toward truth. Pause. Reflect. Ask yourself:

Am I truly on the Lord's side?

Is God pleased to dwell in me?

"You are no longer strangers…you are fellow citizens…being built into a dwelling of God in the Spirit." — Ephesians 2:19–22

We are not just attendees—we are temples. God desires to inhabit us with His Spirit. But He will not dwell where compromise reigns.

Christ at the Center of Scripture

All of Scripture points to Jesus. The first prophecy in Genesis 3:15 foretells His victory over Satan:

"He shall bruise your head, and you shall bruise His heel." —Genesis 3:15 (AMP)

This is the first Gospel announcement. From Genesis to Revelation, the path to the Redeemer unfolds. See: Isaiah 9:6, Matthew 1:23, Luke 1:31, Romans 16:20, Galatians 4:4, Revelation 12:17.

Jesus is not a footnote. He is the headline. The centerpiece. The answer.

Jesus: The Way, Truth, and Life

Jesus declared:

"I am the way, and the truth, and the life. No one comes to the Father except through Me." —John 14:6

Yet today, His name is scarcely mentioned—even in churches. Instead, we hear worldly solutions, political rhetoric, and human philosophies. History shows that when Christianity partners with worldly systems, corruption follows. This is going on right now in the U.S.A.

We are the Church. Our allegiance is to Jesus. We represent Him as revealed in Scripture. What does that look like in a nutshell? Simply this,

"In everything, treat people the same way you want them to treat you…" Matthew 7:12
This is called the Golden Rule. If applied, it would flood the world with justice, mercy, love, and forgiveness. Jesus defeated Satan at the cross by living by those powerful principles.

"Some trust in chariots and some in horses, but we will remember and trust in the name of the Lord our God." — Psalm 20:7 (AMP)

Our Call to Imitate Christ

How are we imitating Christ in the world?

- Is our behavior marked by holiness?

- Is our speech seasoned with grace?

- Are our actions rooted in love?

Let the Holy Spirit speak to you. Let the Word of God transform you—just as it did the early Believers who followed Christ even unto death.

"All Scripture is inspired by God and profitable for teaching, for reproof, for correction, for training in righteousness." —2 Timothy 3:16

The time for passive Christianity is over. Let us return to the Word, to the Son, and to the Spirit who dwells within us. May we be found faithful—not just in belief, but in obedience.

The Consequence of Disobedience

Sin entered through a deceptive voice—one that questioned God's integrity and intentions. Adam and Eve's failure to obey God's command shifted the course of humanity. But even in judgment, God revealed His grace: a covering, a promise, and the beginning of redemption.

"Also for Adam and his wife the Lord God made tunics of skin, and clothed them." (Genesis 3:21)

This was more than a garment—it was a prophetic glimpse of the Lamb who would come.

Prayer

Lord, we come to You acknowledging our need to hear and heed Your Word and also to obey it completely. Forgive us for choosing to walk in our own ways. Teach us to cherish every part of the Scriptures that we might live by Your commands in humility, integrity, and boldness.

May everything we do—speech, action, relationships, and priorities—reflect the character of Jesus. Fill our heart with compassion for those who do not yet know You and give us courage to faithfully share Your Gospel with them.

Holy Spirit, make your home in us and change our hearts so that we shall walk in truth, justice, and love. Empower us to be faithful witnesses and obedient servants to stand up for Your Kingdom until we hear, one day, the words, "Well done, good and faithful servant."

In Jesus' name. Amen.

Reflective Questions

1. In what areas of your life do you struggle to listen, heed, and obey God's Word?

   _____

   _____

   _____

   _____

2. How can you begin to remove personal agendas that hinder your obedience to God?

   _____

   _____

   _____

   _____

3. Are there any prejudices or biases in your heart that you need to repent of?

   _____

   _____

   _____

   _____

4. Do your judgments toward others align with God's Word in all areas?

_____

_____

_____

_____

5. How are you representing Christ in your behavior, speech, and actions before a watching world?

_____

_____

_____

_____

6. What practical step can you take this week to embrace God's Word more fully?

_____

_____

_____

_____

Chapter 3
The Legacy of Faithful Witnesses

In the 21st-century Church, we must remember the fierce battles fought by early believers to preserve the faith, spread the Gospel, and establish the Church. After the deaths of the twelve apostles, the torch was passed to courageous men and women who refused to let the flame of truth die.

Among them was **Polycarp**, a disciple of the Apostle John, who stood firm against heresies and suffered martyrdom for Christ. The early Church Fathers laid theological foundations that still support the Church today. Later, reformers like **Martin Luther** risked their lives to translate the Bible into languages the common people could understand, tearing down barriers between God's Word and His people.

Missionaries ventured into foreign lands, enduring hardship to proclaim the Gospel. In the 18th century, the **Great Awakenings**—led by revivalists such as **George Whitefield**, **John Wesley**, **Jonathan Edwards**, and later

Charles Finney—ignited spiritual renewal across a young America. Their preaching stirred hearts, convicted souls, and changed the course of history.

What united these spiritual giants? A burning zeal to preach the Gospel and teach others to live as followers of Christ. In 1741, **Jonathan Edwards** delivered his famous sermon, *"Sinners in the Hands of an Angry God,"* which pierced even the hardest hearts and brought deep conviction.

In the 20th and early 21st centuries, preachers like **Smith Wigglesworth**, **William Seymour**, **F.F. Bosworth**, **Billy Graham**, **Lester Sumrall**, **Kathryn Kuhlman**, **Oral Roberts**, **Kenneth Hagin**, and **Reinhard Bonnke** carried the torch forward. They emphasized the power of the Holy Spirit, the urgency of the Gospel, and the call to holy living. They held fast to the Word of God and inspired millions.

Today, we must ask: What are these faithful witnesses in heaven saying about the Church today? Who among us walks in their anointing and power?

A Gospel That Must Still Be Preached

John 3:16 reminds us:

"For God so loved the world that He gave His only

begotten Son, that whoever believes in Him should not perish but have everlasting life."

The Greek word for *perish*—**apóllymi**—means to destroy entirely. This is the fate of those who reject the Gospel. The Church must continue its mission until Christ returns.

Charles Spurgeon once said:

"If sinners be damned, at least let them leap to Hell over our dead bodies. And if they perish, let them perish with our arms wrapped about their knees, imploring them to stay. If Hell must be filled, let it be filled in the teeth of our exertions, and let not one go unwarned and unprayed for."

This is the heart of the Gospel: relentless love and unwavering urgency. Every believer, every church, and every ministry must make the spreading of the Gospel and the establishment of God's Kingdom their primary mission.

A Call to Reflect

Children of God, we've inherited victories won by faithful saints—but have we used them to advance God's Kingdom or for personal gain? Let us return to the Word of God, our divine instruction manual for life.

2 Timothy 3:16–17 declares:

[16] *"All Scripture is given by inspiration of God, and is profitable for doctrine, for reproof, for correction, for instruction in righteousness,* [17] *that the man of God may be complete, thoroughly equipped for every good work."*

"Let your heart therefore be loyal to the Lord our God, to walk in His statutes and keep His commandments..."
—1 Kings 8:61

This is our call today: to walk in loyalty, obedience, and faith. Not to point fingers or assign blame, but to reflect, repent, and rise.

Prayer

O, Lord, Incline our hearts, to walk in Your ways not only in easiness but in difficulty as well. Give us hearts that love obedience, hunger for righteousness, and thirst after Your truth. Let Your words mold our desires, not the world. Help us to live with faith, that faith that endures adversity and abides in Your unchanging promises. Like saints before us, help us to persevere with faith in You who is the rewarder of those who seek you.

Teach us to cherish and hold fast to Your promises. Bring to mind the truth when deception ranges about us. Give us strength and refuge when we are weary. Let our lives reflect Your grace and proclaim Your Gospel in a world longing for light. Forgive our complacency. Bring to life once again our first love. Stir in us that holy passion to serve wholeheartedly, for eternity is at stake.

Make us useful to Your Kingdom. Open our eyes, even to service and witnessing. Fill us with Your Spirit. May Your Word direct every step we take. In the midst of the noise, help us to listen to Your voice. May we become doers of this Word, and walk as Jesus did, in obedience and truth, for Your glory.

May this be done in Jesus' name. Amen.

Reflective Questions

1. Am I continuing the legacy of the early believers with the same zeal?

   _____

   _____

   _____

   _____

2. In what ways have I prioritized personal comfort over Kingdom mission?

   _____

   _____

   _____

   _____

3. Do I truly believe God will keep His promises to me?

   _____

   _____

   _____

   _____

Challenge:

Select one person this week with whom you can share your testimony or the Gospel. Pray for them, speak life to them, and show the love of Christ through action.

Chapter 4
God's Will for Humanity

From the opening pages of *Genesis* to the final words of *Revelation*, God unveils His heart for humanity—a divine blueprint etched into creation itself. He didn't just form the world; He formed us for relationship, purpose, and glory.

Picture Eden: a garden untouched by sin, where God walked and talked with Adam and Eve. They weren't just caretakers—they were image-bearers, entrusted with dominion, creativity, and communion with their Creator.

Genesis 1:26–28
"Then God said, 'Let Us make man in Our image, according to Our likeness...'
So God created man in His image...male and female He created them.
Then God blessed them, and said, 'Be fruitful and multiply; fill the earth and subdue it; have dominion...'"

This wasn't a casual suggestion. It was a divine commission—an invitation to partner with God in stewarding His creation.

Choosing Truth or Deception

When God speaks, things happen.

"Let there be light," and there was light.
"Let the waters be gathered," and dry land appeared.
"Let Us make man," and humanity came into being.

Genesis 1:3-30 (Read full chapter)

God's Word is not passive—it's active, creative, and final. Every syllable carries authority. And yet, into this perfect world, God introduced something extraordinary: choice.

He gave Adam and Eve the freedom to obey or rebel. Why? Because love without choice isn't love—it's control. But with choice comes risk. And into that risk slithered a voice. Satan, through the serpent, asked the woman if God indeed said not to eat of every tree in the garden. See Gen. 2:16-17, 3:1-24. The serpent didn't roar. He whispered, "Has God indeed said...?" (Genesis 3:1) That question still echoes today. Satan didn't need to overpower Eve—he only needed to plant doubt. He questioned God's truth, motives, and goodness. He offered a counterfeit promise: "You'll be like God." Sound familiar?

The tactics haven't changed. The enemy still whispers

lies that appeal to our flesh, our pride, our fears. He still tempts us to trade obedience for autonomy, truth for convenience, purpose for pleasure.

So we must ask ourselves: **Whose voice are we listening to? What lies have we accepted as truth? Are we living out our divine assignment—or drifting from it?**

Satan Exposed

Satan's name reveals his nature. The Hebrew word Satan means adversary, accuser, and one who opposes. In the Old Testament, Satan is often used as a title rather than a proper noun. In the New Testament, Satan is referred to as a personal diabolical figure called the Devil (Greek: diabolos), meaning "slanderer" or "accuser." Once an anointed cherub, he fell through pride (Isaiah 14:13–14; Ezekiel 28:1; 1 Tim 3:6). He is also called "the dragon," "the old serpent" (Rev 12:9; 20:2); "the prince of this world" (Jn 12:31; 14:30); "the prince of the power of the air" (Eph 2:2); "the god of this world" (2 Cor. 4:4); "the spirit that now works in the children of disobedience" (Eph 2:2). He is "Beelzebub, the prince of the devils" (Mat 12:24).

He is "the constant enemy of the followers of Christ, and of all truth; full of falsehood and all malice, and seduces to do evil in every possible way." Christians are warned against his "devices" (2 Cor. 2:11), and called on to "resist" him (Jam 4:7). He will do anything in his power to oppose God's people and plans. However, here is the good news: Satan's destiny is sealed—an eternity in the lake of fire (Rev. 20:10).

The Plan of Redemption

Sin didn't surprise God. He already had a plan. After Adam and Eve fell, two realities emerged:

1. **Spiritual death**—separation from God's presence (John 4:24)

2. **Blood sacrifice**—a slain animal to cover their shame

"For as in Adam all die, so also in Christ all will be made alive." (1 Corinthians 15:22)

This was the beginning of the **Plan of Redemption**—a divine rescue mission that culminated in Jesus Christ. Through His blood, atonement for sin was satisfied, and fellowship with God was made available.

God's original instructions still stand:

- **Be fruitful and multiply--prosper in growth and increase.**

- **Fill the earth and subdue it**—bring order, cultivate, govern

- **Have dominion**—exercise authority. God gave every person born in this world the responsibility to take care of the earth He gave them. I encourage you to hold onto this truth, for it's central to understanding what has gone wrong up to the day that we're living in. For you see, God provided a perfect sacrifice 4000 years later to provide redemption for the fall of humanity, providing a way to get back in relationship and fellowship with HIM.

This isn't just ancient history—it's our present calling. We must return to the complete counsel of God's Word—not cherry-picked verses, not cultural interpretations, but the full, unfiltered truth. Our purpose hasn't changed. Our assignment remains.

Choosing the Right Plan to Follow

"For God so loved the world that He gave His only begotten Son, that whoever believes in Him should not perish but have everlasting life." (John 3:16)

The word *"whoever"* is radical. It means no one is excluded. Every soul is a potential heir of salvation. That's why we must treat every person as a future son or daughter of God.

A Call to Accountability

Let's be honest: The Church hasn't always reflected Christ well.

During the COVID-19 pandemic, many lives were lost—not just to disease, but to division and hatred, political and religious corruption, misinformation, and indifference. Bodies were stored in refrigerated trailers due to lack of space. Families were torn apart. Devastating times like this, should be the Church's finest hour to represent God's love for humanity. We must lovingly hold each other accountable for bringing reproach to the name of the Lord, His Word, and the Church.

What will Jesus say about our response?

Romans 2:4 asks: "Do you despise the riches of His goodness...not knowing that the goodness of God leads you to repentance?"

We must confront the corruption, the injustice, the apathy. Not with condemnation—but with conviction. With love. With truth.

Recommitment to God's Will

Let us fulfill our original assignment—not out of obligation, but out of love.

Let us recommit to the Word of God as our final authority. Let us reject the lies of the enemy and confidently live for God's purposes while on earth. Let us treat every soul as a worthy candidate for salvation. Let us fulfill our original assignment—not out of obligation, but out of a heart of obedience.

Prayer

Dear Lord, align our aspirations with Your plans, removing any hurdles in our path with You. Fill us with Your Spirit to walk with courage, humility, and faithfulness. Lead us in truth, let us fight against lies, and grant us the grace to speak boldly when necessary. May Your Word be our foundation and compass.

And let us be filled with Your love and be like Your Son to the rest of the world, tender toward the lost, serving with the broken, and shining in the darkness. Give us the strength to follow You boldly, even when it costs our lives. Unite us as Your Church, faithful in truth, steadfast in love, and rich in good works. In this way, may our lives glorify Your name and direct others toward the hope we have in Christ.

In Jesus' name, Amen.

Reflective Questions

1. Whose voice am I listening to?

_____

_____

_____

2. Am I walking in God's original assignment for my life?

_____

_____

_____

3. How can I better reflect God's glory in today's world?

_____

_____

_____

4. Where do I need to repent, realign, and reengage with God's Word?

_____

_____

_____

Chapter 5
Dominion and Destiny

From Adam and Eve forward, all their descendants received a divine privilege and responsibility: **dominion**. God ordained that every person reflect His glory through this assignment. To resist or hinder the fulfillment of His Word is sin.

Genesis 4:7 shows God's warning to Cain:

"...Sin lies at the door. And its desire is for you, but you should rule over it."

Cain, in jealous rage, killed Abel—violating God's design for life, family, and dominion. In judgment, God cursed him to a life of wandering. Yet even through rebellion, God's purpose pressed forward.

The Tragedy of Cain and the Rise of Seth

Though Cain failed to lead in righteousness, God appointed another seed—**Seth**—to continue the godly lineage.

Genesis 4:25–26:

"…God has appointed another seed for me instead of Abel… Then men began to call on the name of the Lord."

Where one lineage faltered, another was formed to pursue worship, prayer, and right living. The Church today carries this same call: to lead generations toward God through the power of the Holy Spirit—not control or manipulation.

Atonement and the Flood—Resetting the Earth's Mandate

Wickedness multiplied until God sent a global flood, sparing only **Noah**, his family, and select animals. Noah and his family were spared because he lived right. Gen. 6: 9, These are *the records of* the generations (family history) of Noah. *Noah was a righteous man [one who was just and had right standing with God], blameless in his [evil] generation; Noah walked (lived) [in habitual fellowship] with God.* After the flood, God re-established His dominion plan.

Genesis 9:1–7 (NLT):

"Be fruitful and multiply. Fill the earth… All the animals… I have placed them in your power… For God made human beings in His own image."

God's blessing echoed the mandate first given in Eden.

37

Life, family, and stewardship remained central to His design.

God Has Spoken—The Family Matters

From the beginning, family multiplication was God's method to fill the earth with purpose. The enemy seeks to disrupt this structure, but God's design is still sacred. Every household bears spiritual potential. Every life matters.

God of All Souls

Ezekiel 18:4 declares:

"Behold, all souls are Mine... The soul who sins shall die."

The neglect of the oppressed is not merely irresponsible—it is detestable to God. Justice is a spiritual mandate, not a social option.

Proverbs 31:8–9 commands the righteous to "Open your mouth for the speechless... judge righteously... plead the cause of the poor and needy." The Church must rediscover this charge—resisting the cultural trends that numb our spiritual sensitivity. If we are truly ambassadors of Christ, we must reflect His justice in how we speak, vote, disciple, and serve.

The Church must repent. Hypocrisy, corruption, and compromise must be exposed and uprooted. Now is the time to be a mouthpiece of truth—not an echo of culture. We must each ask: Are we advancing God's dominion with justice and love, or are we enabling systems that grieve His heart? Are we part of the solution—or part of the problem?

Human beings are made in the image of God—not to have dominion over each other, but to honor and respect one another.

God's Heart for Justice

Scripture speaks more often about justice for the poor than praise for the wealthy. James 2:5–9:

5 Listen, my beloved brethren: Has God not chosen the poor of this world to be rich in faith and heirs of the kingdom which He promised to those who love Him? 6 But you have dishonored the poor man. Do not the rich oppress you and drag you into the courts? 7 Do they not blaspheme that noble name by which you are called? 8 If you really fulfill the royal law according to the Scripture, "You shall love your neighbor as yourself," you do well; 9 but if you show partiality, you commit sin, and are convicted by the law as transgressors.

Ezekiel 16:49–50 further exposes this injustice with the sin of Sodom:

"…pride, fullness of food… abundance of idleness… neither did she strengthen the hand of the poor and needy."

God is clear: neglect of the poor or oppressed is detestable. Justice is a spiritual mandate.

The Church must rediscover this charge—resisting the cultural trends that numb our spiritual sensitivity. If we are truly ambassadors of Christ, we must reflect His justice in how we speak, vote, disciple, and serve.

A Prophetic Warning

The Great Depression of 1929 ushered in widespread global hardship: stock crashes, trade wars, unemployment, and social unrest. We see similar trends today—moral collapse, economic instability, pride masking vulnerability. Nations forget their frailty. Proverbs 16:18 warns:

"Pride goes before destruction, and a haughty spirit before a fall."

Prayer

Lord God, Creator of all souls, You have entrusted the earth to mankind not to control each other but to steward creation and reflect Your justice and mercy. Forgive us, O God, for failing the second greatest commandment: loving our neighbors as ourselves. Cleanse us from pride, indifference, and hypocrisy. Teach us to open our mouths for those who have no voice, strengthen the hand of the poor, and walk humbly before You. May Your Church rise as a beacon of truth, love, and righteousness in this generation.

Amen.

Reflective Questions

1. Do I put others' destinies on hold because of jealousy, fear, or competition?

_____

_____

_____

_____

2. How am I contributing to God's purpose through my family and relationships?

_____

_____

_____

_____

3. In which ways are God's justice reflected in my heart toward the needy and oppressed?

_____

_____

_____

_____

Chapter 6
The Voice of the Prophets – God's Unyielding Communication to Humanity

"Long ago, God spoke many times and in many ways to our ancestors through the prophets." —Hebrews 1:1

From the beginning, despite humanity's fall into sin and rebellion, God pursued His divine purpose using chosen vessels. The thread of redemption wove through Noah, Abraham's lineage, and the emerging nation of Israel—a people set apart for His glory.

Prophetic Voices: The Mouthpieces of Heaven

God used prophets not only to lead Israel but also to declare His will, reveal mysteries, and confront injustice. From Moses the Lawgiver, Deborah the judge and prophetess, to Samuel the priest and prophet—each carried the weight of divine truth. Other prophets were:

1. Major and Minor Prophets: Isaiah, Jeremiah, Ezekiel, Malachi, and others guided Israel and rebuked

neighboring nations.

2. Prophets to Gentile Nations: Jonah to Nineveh, Ezekiel to Tyre and Egypt, Jeremiah to Babylon.

The Hebrew word for prophet is *nabi, which* means "to bubble forth" like a fountain. Prophets overflowed with God's Word, confronting kings, calling out sin, and imparting hope. They didn't speak out of personal ambition—they were compelled by divine commission. (See Isaiah 1:18–20; Jeremiah 1:4–10; Romans 1:1)

God instituted three major leadership roles to lead Israel:

- Kings led and enforced the law.

- Priests mediated between God and the people.

- Prophets called both to account under God's covenant.

Prophecy: Evidence of God's Sovereignty

One-third of Scripture is prophetic, and many prophecies have been fulfilled with astonishing detail. Isaiah prophesied Christ's birth and crucifixion 700 years in advance (Isaiah 7:14; 9:6; 53:4–8). The genealogy in Luke 3 links Jesus back to Adam, underscoring God's redemptive plan across generations.

These aren't mythological tales—they're backed by historical evidence, archaeological findings, and fulfillment that span centuries. Ezekiel's vision of Israel's regathering found stunning fulfillment in 1948, after nearly two millennia of dispersion.

The High Cost of a True Prophet

God's prophets rarely delivered comfortable words. They bore the burden of rejection, persecution, and death. As Jesus said in Matthew 23:34, some will be scourged, others crucified, for speaking truth in defiance of corrupted systems. Today, prophetic voices still echo—called by God, not by popularity.

May the Lord strengthen and protect His servants who boldly proclaim His Word, unafraid of the cost. (See 1 Peter 3:13–17)

More Voices of the Prophetic: Carriers of God's Word

Beyond the well-known figures like Moses, Deborah, and Samuel, Scripture introduces us to many others who faithfully echoed God's heart:

Even among the early Church, prophecy continued as a

gift of the Spirit—used to edify, exhort, encourage the Body of Christ (1 Corinthians 14:1–5).

Wake Up, Church! Return to His Voice

Despite invasions, exiles, and rebellion, Israel remains. God's covenant still stands. Deuteronomy 28 lays it bare—obedience brings blessing, disobedience invites curses. God's dealings with Israel should awaken nations today.

There's a spiritual war raging: light vs. darkness, truth vs. lies. The Church must arise—not with politics, cultural ungodliness or compromised alliances—but with purity, prayer, and proclamation.

Ask yourself:

- Where is Jesus being exalted?

- Where is the Gospel advancing?

- Where is obedience prevailing?

Let our boast be in Jesus alone. "Let's Make Jesus Great"—not as a slogan, but a lifestyle that reflects Him.

A Remnant Preserved

God has always kept a remnant. Elijah believed he was alone, yet God revealed 7,000 faithful ones (1 Kings 18). Today, the remnant still stands—the Church of Jesus Christ, faithful and unbowed to the gods of this world.

We are God's army—not of flesh and politics—but of Spirit and Truth. 1 Corinthians 15:57 declares: "But thanks be to God, who gives us the victory through our Lord Jesus Christ."

Prayer

Lord God Almighty, clear every distraction, every fear, and spiritual dullness from us that keeps us from knowing Your will in this urgent hour. Open our ears, eyes, and spirits to Your truth and leading.

Help us honor Your Word above all else. Grant us the courage to stand for truth and live in a manner reflecting Your holiness and grace. Create within us the hearts of repenters, who turn quickly away from sin and are eager to live in right standing.

Consider us part of the remnant who persevere, hold fast, and devote themselves fully to You. As Your Church, give us the strength to shine brightly, to proclaim Jesus boldly, to accomplish our mission without compromise. We give ourselves over to You and trust You for victory.

This we ask in the powerful name of Jesus Christ. Amen.

Reflective Questions

1. Am I more concerned with cultural approval than obedience to God's truth?

_____

_____

_____

_____

2. Do I honor God's prophetic voice in my life through Scripture, godly counsel, or the conviction of the Holy Spirit?

_____

_____

_____

_____

3. How do I respond when God's Word challenges my comfort or convicts my lifestyle?

_____

_____

_____

_____

Chapter 7
Prophetic Parallels — Echoes into Our Age

"Surely the Lord God does nothing, unless He reveals His secret to His servants the prophets." —Amos 3:7

The prophets of old were not detached mystics whispering in obscurity. They were bold voices in turbulent times—challengers of kings, defenders of truth, and bearers of God's heart. Their messages pierced culture, confronted compromise, and summoned a nation back to the living God.

Today, those voices echo through Scripture and history, calling the Church into alignment with heaven's will. As spiritual climates shift and nations tremble, the mantle of the prophets still falls on those willing to speak on God's behalf.

Prophetic Lives with Modern Relevance

Nathan: Confronting Sin Behind Closed Doors

Nathan's rebuke of King David (2 Samuel 12) wasn't just courageous—it was restorative.

Today: Leaders and believers alike need accountability and prophetic correction to uphold holiness in private and public life.

Elijah: Challenging the Culture of Idolatry

In an age when Baal was worshipped, Elijah boldly declared, "How long will you waver between two opinions?" (1 Kings 18:21).
Today: Prophets call the Church out of compromise—away from celebrity obsession, prosperity distortions, and lukewarm faith—and back into covenant fidelity.

Daniel: Thriving Without Bowing

Daniel served faithfully in Babylon without defiling himself (Daniel 1:8–21).
Today: Christians must stand unshaken in secular workplaces, political realms, and academic systems—bold but gracious witnesses of truth.

Amos & Micah: Prophets of Justice

Amos denounced exploitation; Micah demanded justice, mercy, and humility (Micah 6:8).
Today: Prophetic voices speak against racial injustice, poverty, corruption, and policies that dishonor God's image in humanity.

Hosea: Love That Redeems

His painful yet purposeful marriage mirrored God's relentless love for a wayward people.

Today: Prophetic lives demonstrate the cost of love—persisting with mercy, even when betrayed by those they minister to.

John the Baptist: Prepare the Way!

His message was simple but seismic: Repent, for the Kingdom is near (Matthew 3:2).

Today: Prophetic messengers urge readiness for Christ's return—calling out distractions, false teachings, and lukewarmness.

Prophetic Warfare in Today's Church

True prophets do not cater to applause. Their assignment often invites rejection and suffering. Yet their words anchor the Church in times of shaking. From pandemics to moral decline, war to spiritual apathy, God is raising bold voices to speak:

- Messages of repentance instead of popularity.

- Calls for holiness instead of compromise.

- Declarations of truth amid a flood of lies.

As Jesus warned in Matthew 23:34, prophetic ministry often bears a cross. Yet through that sacrifice, God births revival and restoration.

Where Are Today's Prophets?

- Are we listening for God's voice or silencing it with comfort?

- Are we lifting the name of Jesus or amplifying worldly agendas?

- Are we preparing the Bride of Christ or entertaining the masses?

The challenge isn't whether God is speaking—but whether we're hearing and obeying.

A Remnant with Resolve

Just as God preserved 7,000 faithful followers in Elijah's time (1 Kings 19:18), He is raising a remnant today—bold believers who have not bowed to Baal or kissed the idols of this age.

This remnant isn't defined by popularity, but by purity. Not by influence, but by intimacy. They are torchbearers in the dark, commissioned to speak light into confusion, hope into despair, and truth into deception.

As we reflect on the prophetic voices that shaped Israel's destiny—from Moses to Malachi—we recognize that their messages were not bound to ancient history. Their assignments carried echoes of God's heart that still resound today. The prophetic mantle didn't disappear with the closing of the Old Testament; it was fulfilled in Christ and now continues through those who yield to His Spirit.

In our present generation, where spiritual compromise and cultural confusion abound, the need for prophetic clarity is more urgent than ever. We must listen not just to what the prophets said, but discern how their lives speak into the call of the Church today.

Prayer

Lord, we humble ourselves before You. Forgive us for any unbelief, resistance, or fear concerning Your gifts. Remove anything that hinders us from fully embracing the work of the Holy Spirit.

Teach us to walk in humility, discernment, and love. Help us to honor and steward the gifts You've given, not for self-gain, but for building up Your Church and Your Kingdom. Raise up true apostles, prophets, and Spirit-led believers who will lead with truth, boldness, and grace.

Make us faithful and obedient vessels, ready to be used for Your glory. We receive your power and lead with gratitude and reverence.

In Jesus' name, Amen.

Journal

Write about how you have seen God use spiritual gifts in you or someone else during the spiritual journey. Ask the Holy Spirit to reveal areas where you may need to grow in discernment, boldness, or humility.

_____

_____

_____

_____

_____

_____

_____

_____

_____

_____

_____

_____

_____

_____

_____

_____

_____

_____

Chapter 8
The Voice of the Son: God's Final Word to Humanity

Hebrews 1:1–3

"God, who at various times and in various ways spoke in time past to the fathers by the prophets, has in these last days spoken to us by His Son, whom He has appointed heir of all things, through whom also He made the worlds; who being the brightness of His glory and the express image of His person, and upholding all things by the word of His power, when He had by Himself purged our sins, sat down at the right hand of the Majesty on high."

What a powerful declaration from God the Father about His Son, Jesus Christ—Savior of the world and the promised seed of the woman. Though sin entered the world through Adam, eternal life came through Christ. The contrast is staggering, and the victory is glorious.

The Contrast Between Adam and Christ

Romans 5:17–19 AMP

"For if by the trespass of the one (Adam), death reigned...
much more surely will those who receive the abundance of
grace and the free gift of righteousness reign in [eternal] life
through the One, Jesus Christ.

...Through one act of righteousness there resulted
justification of life to all men.

...Through the obedience of the one Man the many will be
made righteous and acceptable to God."

Adam's failure brought condemnation. Christ's
obedience brought justification.

Through Jesus, we are not only forgiven—we are made
righteous and restored to right standing with God.

The Joy of Believing

What Christ accomplished at Calvary is the greatest
cause for celebration in human history. He was the sacrificial
Lamb, crucified for our sins, and raised in power. I remember
a song we used to sing:

"Jesus, I'll Never Forget What You've Done for Me."

To this day, my soul and spirit continue to magnify the
Lord.

Mary, the mother of Jesus, understood this joy. When
she visited her cousin Elizabeth, who was pregnant with

John the Baptist, she sang a song of praise that still echoes through generations:

Luke 1:46–55

"My soul magnifies the Lord,

And my spirit has rejoiced in God my Savior...

He who is mighty has done great things for me,

And holy is His name...

He has exalted the lowly...

He has helped His servant Israel...

As He spoke to our fathers,

To Abraham and to his seed forever."

Authority Over the Enemy

We say we believe God's promises—but do we live like Jesus is the Champion, the Conqueror, the Hero who defeated the kingdom of darkness?

Jesus declared:

Luke 10:18–19

"I saw Satan fall like lightning from heaven.

Behold, I give you the authority to trample on serpents and scorpions, and over all the power of the enemy, and nothing shall by any means hurt you."

We don't just have salvation—we have authority.

We are empowered to overcome every attack of the enemy.

A Personal Testimony

Years ago, when my husband was away on an Air Force mission, I faced a spiritual battle. One night, while my daughters slept, a spirit of fear filled my bedroom. I cried out to the Lord for help. He instructed me to go downstairs—into the dark—and march around the four large rooms of our home seven times, speaking in tongues aloud. As soon as I opened my mouth, courage surged through me. The atmosphere shifted. God's presence filled every corner of our home. I marched back upstairs and slept in peace.

We serve a mighty God who equips us to overcome every attack.

When the enemy tempts us to compromise, we must rebuke him and obey the Lord.

A Word of Caution

It's apparent that many in the "Church" choose to go their way instead of solely following Jesus' righteous path for Kingdom living. Jesus warned us:

Matthew 7:13–14

"Enter by the narrow gate; for wide is the gate and broad is the way that leads to destruction, and there are many who go in by it. Because narrow is the gate and difficult is the way which leads to life, and there are few who find it."

His way is not popular. His path is not easy. But it is the only way that leads to life.

Sadly, many in the Church have chosen the broad way—accommodating personal ideologies, cultural trends, and political agendas. The spirit of antichrist has infiltrated pulpits and pews alike, twisting Scripture to fit human preferences.

Misrepresenting the Messiah

Some portray Jesus as a militant leader, commanding His followers to take everything by force—even if it means inciting division or violence. But this is not the Jesus of Scripture.

When Peter drew his sword during Jesus' arrest, Jesus rebuked him:

Matthew 26:52
"Put away your sword," Jesus told him.
"Those who use the sword will die by the sword."

Jesus didn't come to force allegiance. He came to offer love, truth, and redemption.

Even Napoleon Bonaparte recognized this:

"Alexander, Caesar, Charlemagne, and I have founded empires. But on what did we rest the creations of our genius? Jesus Christ founded His empire upon love, and at this hour, millions of men would die for Him."

Now, Church—it's time to make it available again to the world. Let us proclaim the Gospel boldly. Let us walk in love and truth. Let us live as citizens of the Kingdom, ambassadors of Christ, and stewards of His glory.

Prayer

Lord Jesus, thank You for the victory You won at Calvary. Help us to walk boldly in the authority You have given us. Strengthen us to reject fear, compromise, and deception. So we can walk the narrow path, which is not an easy task.

Clean our hearts, align our minds with Your truth, and use us as vessels of Your love, power, and holiness. Let our lives bring glory to the name of Jesus.

In Jesus' name, Amen.

Reflective Questions

1. In what areas of my life am I still living in fear or compromising my spiritual values?

_____

_____

_____

_____

Challenge #1:

Review your recent actions, habits, and words. Do they align with God's truth, or with cultural narratives? Make at least one intentional change this week to reflect God's Word more fully.

Challenge #2:

Set aside time to pray through your home. Walk from room to room, speak Scripture, and invite the Holy Spirit to reign over your household.

Chapter 9
The Living Word: Fueling the Fire of Faith

Imagine adding kindling to a dwindling fire—the flames revive as if they never died down. That's what happens when we read, study, and meditate on God's Word. Our faith ignites. Our love intensifies. Our zeal to do His will is renewed.

Hebrews 4:12
"For the word of God is quick, and powerful, and sharper than any two-edged sword,
piercing even to the dividing asunder of soul and spirit, and of the joints and marrow,
and is a discerner of the thoughts and intents of the heart."

God's Word is alive. It doesn't just inform—it transforms. It reveals who He is, what His will is, and what He desires for all. Jesus Christ died for the sins of all so that whoever from all can receive salvation, eternal life, and become part of the family of God. But here's the question:
Who have we excluded from "all"?

Have we reshaped the Gospel to fit our cultural preferences, political ideologies, or personal biases?

The Word Made Flesh

To grasp the magnitude of Jesus Christ's power and divinity, we must believe and receive what He has said about Himself and creation.

Psalm 138:2

"I will worship toward Your holy temple,
And praise Your name For Your lovingkindness and Your truth;
For You have magnified Your word above all Your name."

John 1:1–14 AMP (selected)

"In the beginning was the Word, and the Word was with God, and the Word was God...
All things were made through Him...
In Him was life, and the life was the light of men...
And the Word became flesh and dwelt among us,
and we beheld His glory...full of grace and truth."

Jesus is the Word in flesh. He is Immanuel—God with us (Isaiah 7:14; Matthew 1:23). He is the brightness of God's glory and the express image of His person (Hebrews 1:1–3). All power and authority in heaven and on earth belong to Him (Matthew 28:18). He is the head of the Church. This is powerfully declared in Colossians 1:13-23:

He has delivered us from the power of darkness and conveyed *us* into the kingdom of the Son of His love, [14] in whom we have redemption through His blood, the forgiveness of sins.

[15] He is the image of the invisible God, the firstborn over all creation. [16] For by Him all things were created that are in heaven and that are on earth, visible and invisible, whether thrones or dominions or principalities or powers. All things were created through Him and for Him. [17] And He is before all things, and in Him all things consist. [18] And He is the head of the body, the church, who is the beginning, the firstborn from the dead, that in all things He may have the preeminence.

[19] For it pleased *the Father that* in Him all the fullness should dwell, [20] and by Him to reconcile all things to Himself, by Him, whether things on earth or things in heaven, having made peace through the blood of His cross.

[21] And you, who once were alienated and enemies in your mind by wicked works, yet now He has reconciled [22] in the body of His flesh through death, to present you holy, and blameless, and above reproach in His sight— [23] if indeed you continue in the faith, grounded and steadfast, and are not

moved away from the hope of the gospel which you heard, which was preached to every creature under heaven, of which I, Paul, became a minister.

The Church's Call in the Last Days

We are New Covenant believers, led by the Holy Spirit into all truth. In these last days, nothing is more important than obeying the commands of the Lord.

John 14:6

"I am the way, the truth, and the life.
No one comes to the Father except through Me."

The life and work of Christ must continue through His ecclesia—with boldness and power. We are the Church, and the world will know we are Christians by our love.

John 13:34–35

"A new commandment I give to you, that you love one another;
as I have loved you, that you also love one another.
By this all will know that you are My disciples, if you have love for one another."

Confronting Hypocrisy and Injustice

Many Christians believe that opposing abortion and homosexuality absolves them from addressing other sins—

like injustice, greed, or self-indulgence. But Jesus rebuked this kind of selective righteousness.

Matthew 23:23–28 (selected)

"Woe to you, scribes and Pharisees, hypocrites!
For you pay tithe...but have neglected the weightier matters of the law: justice, mercy, and faith...
You cleanse the outside...but inside are full of extortion and self-indulgence...
You appear righteous...but inside are full of hypocrisy and lawlessness."

Justice, mercy, and faith are not optional—they are central to the Gospel.

I once heard a minister say that many Black Christians feel the Church isn't addressing justice issues. Another replied, "Justice for the unborn," and nothing more was said to address the concern of an entire group of God's people. That moment revealed a painful truth: political polarization has infiltrated the Church.

The Church must return to the Word.
The Church must return to God's kind of love.
The Church must return to truth.

Prayer

Oh, Lord God, awaken our appetites to seek after Scripture and meditate on it daily for the renewing of our hearts and minds. Purge our motives and judgments, O Jesus. Come and reveal to us any areas in which we have walked in religious pride, cultural bias, or favoritism. Holy Spirit, lead us into all truth. Awaken our ears to Your voice and give us courage to act, even when the course is contrary to our comfort or culture.

In Jesus' name, Amen.

Ministry Challenge

Set a goal to meditate on and journal through one verse per day from Hebrews, Romans, or John. Let the Word speak to you deeply.

_____

_____

_____

_____

_____

_____

_____

_____

_____

_____

_____

_____

_____

_____

_____

_____

_____

_____

_____

Chapter 10
Listen to Him: The Church's Call to Obey Christ

Matthew 17:5 NASB

"While he was still speaking, a bright cloud overshadowed them, and behold, a voice from the cloud said,

'This is My beloved Son, with whom I am well pleased; listen to Him!'"

We cannot casually read past this divine command. El Shaddai—God Almighty—didn't suggest we listen to Jesus. He commanded it. This is not optional for the Church. It is foundational.

The Greek word for "listen" is *akouō*, meaning:

- To hear and attend to

- To understand and perceive

- To give ear to a teacher

- To comprehend and obey

Listening to Jesus means more than hearing His words—it means aligning our lives with His voice.

Knowing His Voice

John 10:4–5

"And when He brings out His own sheep, He goes before them; and the sheep follow Him, for they know His voice. Yet they will by no means follow a stranger, but will flee from him, for they do not know the voice of strangers."

Jesus makes it clear: His sheep know His voice. They follow Him. They flee from deception. So we must ask if we are truly listening to Jesus—or to the voices of culture, politics, and personal preference? Are we obeying everything He taught—or selectively following what's convenient?

Discerning Kingdom Allegiances

I remember when my family moved to a Southern city and saw a bumper sticker that read **"God-n-Guns."** Given America's history, that message promotes the kingdom of darkness more than the Kingdom of Light. The Body of Christ must be mindful of its associations. If we oppose abortion, we must also oppose gun violence. The Church should advocate for the protection of every life. God's Word—not ungodly cultural slogans—must shape our values.

The Government of Christ

Jesus set the standard for how His Church should implement His Kingdom on earth. He expects us to represent Him, preach about Him, and multiply His followers—regardless of worldly systems.

Isaiah 9:6–7

"For unto us a Child is born...
And the government will be upon His shoulder...
Of the increase of His government and peace there will be no end...
To order it and establish it with judgment and justice...
The zeal of the Lord of hosts will perform this."

As citizens of God's Kingdom, we seek His rule—His judgment and justice. We fill the earth with the knowledge of His glory by imitating Christ and obeying Him. We have no fellowship with ungodliness. We live by faith as ambassadors for Christ (2 Corinthians 5:20).
We continue the greater works He promised (John 14:12).
We shine His light and salt the earth with His goodness and love.

Peter and John Nailed It

Peter and John were arrested for healing a man who had been lame since birth. They boldly declared that it was faith in Jesus' name that made him whole—and they preached the Gospel without apology (Acts 4:1-4).

Isaiah 40:8

"The grass withers, the flower fades,
But the word of our God stands forever."

Matthew 24:35

"Heaven and earth will pass away,
But My words will by no means pass away."

No matter how advanced, wealthy, or powerful the world becomes—God is sovereign. His Word stands. His Son reigns. And His Church must continue the mission.

God has spoken.

Jesus is Lord.

The Church must obey. Let us rise as faithful disciples. Let us preach the Gospel with boldness. Let us live as ambassadors of the Kingdom—until He returns.

Forward, Christian soldiers!

Prayer

Father, may Your Kingdom be manifested through us, in our words, deeds, and mindsets. Where there is strife, turn us into peacemakers. In situations of injustice, grant us the bravery to advocate for what is right. Assist us in recognizing every life, from a child in the womb to older people, as precious in Your eyes. Warm our hearts for the suffering, and allow empathy to inspire us to act. Enable us through Your Spirit to serve as devoted representatives of Christ, spreading light, hope, and justice in every place You guide us. In the name of Jesus, Amen

Reflective Questions

1. What areas of my life reflect obedience to His words?

_____

_____

_____

_____

Challenge #1:

- Write down what you read, watch, and listen to over a few days.
- Ask: Does this content help me hear Jesus better or muffle His voice?

Challenge #2:

Find one way this week to be salt and light (Matthew 5:13-6):

- Feed someone in need.
- Speak up against injustice in love.
- Share the Gospel with someone God puts on your heart.

Chapter 11
Love Is the Measure of Truth

Throughout the Old and New Testaments, God exposes and warns us to watch out for deception, false prophets, and false teachers. Despite the abundance of knowledge, facts, and truth available today, many American citizens—and sadly, many Christians—are deceived. Truth has been traded for agenda. Conviction for compromise.

The Crisis of Disobedience

The spiritual condition of much of Christendom in the U.S. and abroad reveals a failure to be Christlike and obedient to Scripture. This failure has contributed to the moral and societal decline we now witness. Baby boomers and millennials alike have seen institutions once rooted in integrity and law now are compromised by corruption and evil. The mixture of religion and politics has incited hatred, racism, fear, and division—all in the name of influence and votes.

If you struggle to receive unfiltered biblical truth because it challenges your worldview, consider these questions:

- How are the teachings of Jesus Christ being implemented?

- How does this impact the spreading of the Gospel?

- Does it cause oppression or promote righteousness?

- Does it hinder others from fulfilling God's dominion mandate?

- Is love for God and others truly being lived out?

Love Is the Foundation

Many in the Body of Christ are knowledge-heavy but obedience-poor. Biblical knowledge should lead us to know Elohim—our Creator—and reflect His will, plan, and purpose.

Matthew 22:36–40 AMP

"'You shall love the Lord your God with all your heart...
and your neighbor as yourself...
The whole Law and the Prophets depend on these two commandments.'"

John 14:21

"The one who has My commandments and keeps them is the one who loves Me..."

1 John 4:7–11 (selected)

"Beloved, let us love one another, for love is of God...

In this is love, not that we loved God, but that He loved us...

If God so loved us, we also ought to love one another."

What does love have to do with it? EVERYTHING!

Love is not optional. It is the measure of our relationship with God and others.

Matthew 5:43–48 (selected)

"Love your enemies, bless those who curse you...

Pray for those who spitefully use you...

For if you love those who love you, what reward have you?...

Therefore you shall be perfect, just as your Father in heaven is perfect."

We must choose whom we will serve and obey—especially in times of testing. Jesus chose obedience all the time.

John 6:38

"For I have come down from heaven, not to do My own will, but the will of Him who sent Me."

John 4:34

"My food is to do the will of Him who sent Me, and to finish His work."

Matthew 7:21

"Not everyone who says to Me, 'Lord, Lord,' shall enter the kingdom of heaven,

but he who does the will of My Father in heaven."

A Changed Heart

Jeremiah 17:9

"The heart is deceitful above all things, and desperately wicked; who can know it?" The first step to overcoming a wicked heart is to become a new creation in Christ and receive the Holy Spirit.

1 Corinthians 2:12–15 (selected)

"We have received...the Spirit who is from God...

The natural man does not receive the things of the Spirit of God...

But he who is spiritual judges all things..."

Only the Spirit of God can reveal the truth of God.
Only the Spirit of God can convict the heart of sin.

Love's Ultimate Expression

Church, God has Spoken! God is love! To illustrate the extent of His love, John 3:16-17 says,

"16 For God so loved the world that He gave His only begotten Son, that whoever believes in Him should not

perish but have everlasting life. [17] For God did not send His Son into the world to condemn the world, but that the world through Him might be saved."

Oftentimes, many of us only quote verse 16; however, it's verse 17 that shares another important truth that God's people need to hold dear in their hearts. Jesus didn't come to condemn but to save the world. I point this out because we often judge unbelievers harshly instead of praying for their salvation, speaking truth to them, and trusting God to deal with them according to His righteousness and justice. The Holy Spirit is the one who convicts the hearts of humanity. Jesus said He would send the Holy Spirit to convict the world of its sins. John 16:7-10 NLT,

"[7] But in fact, it is best for you that I go away, because if I don't, the Advocate won't come. If I do go away, then I will send him to you. [8] And when he comes, he will convict the world of its sin, and of God's righteousness, and of the coming judgment. [9] The world's sin is that it refuses to believe in me. [10] Righteousness is available because I go to the Father, and you will see me no more."

God is always motivated by love. By His Spirit, we are empowered to:

- Share the Gospel (evangelism)

- Teach others to follow Christ (discipleship)

- Help them walk in dominion (rulership)

- Embrace them as family (relationship)

So, we must ask:

- What do we allow in our hearts that hinders us from loving others to Christ?

- Does the world see love or hate in our lives?

- Do they witness truth or deception, justice or injustice?

Church, God has spoken. God is love. Let us live like it.

Prayer

Jesus, enable us to love our adversaries, assist those in pain, and showcase Your grace in everything we undertake. Transform us into vessels of truth, compassion, and harmony. God, show compassion to our country. Elevate virtuous leaders and bring back justice and harmony in all areas. May Your love dispel fear within us and guide us to be representatives of Your Kingdom.

In the name of Jesus, Amen

Ministry Challenges

1. This week, you are encouraged to pray for an enemy, bless them, and forgive them.

2. Each day for one week, do one intentional act of love toward someone outside your comfort zone.

3. Share a Scripture-based truth on your social media or in a personal conversation, but make sure it's spoken in love, humility, and grace.

Chapter 12
Grab the Baton: Continuing Christ's Mission

If we profess to belong to Jesus, our lives should reflect His life and continue His mission. We pick up where He left off. We grab the baton—the Gospel, the Great Commission—and run with it as His disciples and His Church.

Matthew 16:15–18

"He said to them, 'But who do you say that I am?'
Simon Peter answered and said, 'You are the Christ, the Son of the living God.'
Jesus answered and said to him, 'Blessed are you, Simon Bar-Jonah, for flesh and blood has not revealed this to you, but My Father who is in heaven.
And I also say to you that you are Peter, and on this rock I will build My Church, and the gates of Hades shall not prevail against it.'"

Peter's confession of faith is the foundation of the Church. Jesus is the *petra*—the bedrock, the cornerstone.

We, as "living stones," are built upon Him (1 Peter 2:5–6).

The Voice of the Church

The Lord's Church is the institution that upholds righteousness and justice and brings God's favor over a nation.

Proverbs 14:34 NLT

"Righteousness exalts a nation, but sin is a disgrace to any people."

Deuteronomy 4:7–8 AMP

"What great nation has a god so near...
Or statutes and judgments so righteous as this whole law...?"

These truths are fulfilled in Jesus Christ—King of kings, Lord of lords, and the embodiment of God's Law.

Jesus is the Answer for the World Today

The Gospel of Jesus Christ is the transformational message that holds back darkness and evil. The New Testament is our guidebook for living like Christ. The Old Testament is our foundation and foreshadowing of His work.

Romans 15:4

"Whatever things were written before were written for our learning..."

Luke 24:27

"Beginning at Moses and all the Prophets, He expounded...the things concerning Himself."

Sadly, some use the Old Testament to justify rebellion, revenge, and hypocrisy. But Jesus came to fulfill the Law—not to weaponize it.

Imagine the impact if more Christians truly lived as ambassadors of Christ:

- Making disciples of all nations
- Filling the earth with good works
- Setting captives free from oppression

Crime, violence, injustice, and immorality would decrease. Remember, Righteousness exalts a nation. An obedient Church tears down the strongholds of Satan.

The Ten Commandments as Gates

The 10 Commandments are like gates of righteousness that block the flood of corruption, evil, lawlessness, injustice, immorality, etc., which allow the enemy (Satan) to weaken or destroy nations. However, when we ignore them, the gates swing open—and anything can come in. As it pertains to sexual immorality, one of the 10 Commandments says, "Do not commit adultery." The result of not obeying is that all types of sexual sins have increased and become strongholds throughout society. Proper relationships are destroyed (family, marriage, manhood, womanhood, children, community, etc). Keeping the Commandments is evidence that we love and abide in Jesus Christ (1 John 3:24). Jesus said that if we love Him, we will obey His commandments. Love for God and people is the essence of all the commandments in God's Word. God has spoken!

- Are we running with the baton—or dropping it?
- Are we proclaiming truth—or letting lies prevail?
- Are we building on Christ—or compromising with the world?

Let us rise as the Church Jesus died to build.
Let us obey His Word.
Let us exalt His name.
Let us be the voice of righteousness in a world desperate for truth.

Grab the baton. The race is not over.

If we don't, it will be Satan's words that go unchallenged and prevail. The systems of this world are being prepared for the anti-Christ. It's his spirit at work in governments, religion, businesses, economies, families, education, entertainment, and throughout societies. However, 1 John 4:3-4 declares this powerful truth,

"*3 and every spirit that does not confess that Jesus Christ has come in the flesh is not of God. And this is the spirit of the Antichrist, which you have heard was coming, and is now already in the world. 4 You are of God, little children, and have overcome them, because He who is in you is greater than he who is in the world.*"

But thanks *be* to God, who gives us the victory through our Lord Jesus Christ. 1 Cor. 15:57

Prayer

Lord Jesus, thank you for calling us to be Your Church and for placing Your truth in our hands. Empower us with Your Spirit to act courageously, follow the path of righteousness, and communicate truth with love. Utilize us to illuminate Your truth, dispel darkness, and create a lasting influence. Empower us to be steadfast and glorify Your name in everything we undertake.

In the name of Jesus, Amen

Activity

Scripture Meditation:

Memorize or meditate on these verses throughout the week:

- Matthew 16:18: *"...on this rock I will build My Church, and the gates of Hades shall not prevail against it."*
- 1 John 4:4: *"Greater is He who is in you than he who is in the world."*
- Proverbs 14:34: *"Righteousness exalts a nation..."*

Ministry Challenge:

Choose one tangible way to be the voice of the Church this week:

- Share the Gospel with someone in your workplace, school, or neighborhood.
- Post a Bible-based message of hope or truth on social media.
- Volunteer in a ministry that serves your community (homeless outreach, youth mentoring, prison ministry, etc.).
- Start or join a prayer group focused on local and national revival.

Chapter 13
Revival of the Church: A Call to Awaken and Arise

The oracle (a burdensome message—a pronouncement from God) which Habakkuk the prophet saw. O Lord, how long will I call for help And You will not hear? I cry out to You, "Violence!" Yet You do not save. ³ Why do You make me see iniquity, and cause me to look on wickedness? For destruction and violence are before me; Strife continues and contention arises. Therefore, the law is ineffective and ignored And justice is never upheld, For the wicked surround the righteous; Therefore, justice becomes perverted. ⁵ [The Lord replied,] "Look among the nations! See! Be astonished! Wonder! For I am doing something in your days—You would not believe it if you were told. Habakuk 1:1-5

The prophet Habakkuk lamented violence, iniquity, and injustice—so much that the law seemed powerless and justice delayed. God responded with a word of awe:

"Look among the nations...I will work a work in your

93

days..." —Habakkuk 1:5

Today, we echo Habakkuk's cry. We witness corruption, spiritual compromise, and a Church in need of revival. But just as God told Habakkuk to live by faith, so too must we wait on Him and rejoice—even in the midst of terrible circumstances (Habakkuk 3:17–19).

"The just shall live by faith" Hab. 2:4 and wait on God to act 3:17-19, which reads:

"Though the fig tree may not blossom, Nor fruit be on the vines; Though the labor of the olive may fail, And the fields yield no food; Though the flock may be cut off from the fold, And there be no herd in the stalls—[18] *Yet I will rejoice in the Lord, I will joy in the God of my salvation.*[19] *The Lord God is my strength; He will make my feet like deer's feet, and He will make me walk on my high hills."*

My cry to the Lord is for Him to revive the Church so it can be that light of God's glory on the earth. As members of the Body of Christ, the Words of our Lord God should have prominence and precedence over other voices. Amid the national crisis in the U.S. and other nations, we desperately need divine intervention from heaven above. Psalm 20:7 reminds us,

"Some trust in chariots, and some in horses; But we will

remember the name of the Lord our God."

Habakkuk 3:1–2

"O Lord, I have heard Your speech and was afraid;

O Lord, revive Your work in the midst of the years!

In the midst of the years make it known;

In wrath remember mercy."

Two Kingdoms, One Choice

The Garden of Eden exposed two kingdoms at war—one of obedience, one of rebellion.

Yet God is not at war with Satan; He delegated authority on Earth to humanity.

Every life choice declares which kingdom we serve.

Matthew 6:24

"No one can serve two masters; for either he will hate the one and love the other, or else he will be loyal to the one and despise the other. You cannot serve God and mammon."

Mammon represents riches, trust in wealth, and misplaced allegiance.

According to Vine's Expository Dictionary, it is personified—an idol of trust. Every person will either serve God or be seduced by Mammon—the bait of Satan.

The Great Deceiver

Satan deceived Adam and Eve by appealing to their eyes, flesh, and pride.

He still uses these tactics today—offering forbidden fruit while hiding its consequences.

1 John 2:15–17

"Do not love the world...For all that is in the world—

the lust of the flesh, the lust of the eyes, and the pride of life—

is not of the Father...but he who does the will of God abides forever."

John 16:33

"In the world you will have tribulation; but be of good cheer, I have overcome the world."

1 John 5:4

"For whatever is born of God overcomes the world.

And this is the victory...our faith."

God Still Provides

It is God's will that His people look to Him for everything—even wealth.

Deuteronomy 8:18

"Remember the Lord your God...for it is He who gives you

power to get wealth..."

Look at Daniel: taken captive into Babylon, he rose to the highest office. He remained righteous and spiritually uncompromised even under a pagan regime.

Daniel rose from captivity in Babylon to promotion to the highest office in the land by Nebuchadnezzar. As a prophet of Israel, he remained faithful and obedient to God's laws and commands while governing a Gentile nation. He didn't let Babylonian rule and culture influence him but maintained his spiritual life amid a heathen environment. When God finally humbled the Babylonian King because of pride, he had these words to say:

"*34 And at the end of the time I, Nebuchadnezzar, lifted my eyes to heaven, and my understanding returned to me; and I blessed the Most High and praised and honored Him who lives forever: For His dominion is an everlasting dominion, and His Kingdom is from generation to generation. 35 All the inhabitants of the earth are reputed as nothing; He does according to His will in the army of heaven and among the inhabitants of the earth. No one can restrain His hand or say to Him, 'What have You done?'"*

Daniel's righteous behavior allowed him to receive wealth, favor, and liberty to receive prophecies for the present and future. Not only that, but He also advised the king to break off his sins by being righteous and his iniquities by showing mercy to the poor. God still provides for His people today. If we seek His Kingdom first and all His righteousness, then the provisions we need we will receive, Matt. 6:33.

Last Days and Present Crisis

Jesus foretold the signs of the last days:

- Wars and rumors of wars

- Nations rising against nations

- Earthquakes, pestilence, famines

- False prophets and deception

(Matthew 24)

We must be vigilant, not passive. The Church must turn away from hypocrisy and unrighteous ways, then God's glory can be seen in a dark world.

But there is a **faithful remnant**—those who obey, proclaim, and endure. It's time for revival.
It's time to rise as the Bride of Christ—pure, obedient, aflame with truth.

Isaiah 60:1–2

"Arise, shine; for your light has come...

Darkness shall cover the Earth...but the Lord will arise upon you."

Let the Church be bold.

Let the Gospel be proclaimed.

Let hearts burn with holy fire.

Prayer

In Your just judgment, Father, keep mercy in mind. Pardon us for relying on earthly systems, comforts, and false idols. We have frequently relied on our own reasoning and connected with perspectives that do not represent You. Sanctify and empower Your Bride, and remove all our unrighteousness. Today, we select You over everything, over wealth, over arrogance, over concession. We reject all loyalty that opposes Your Kingdom. We recommit our lives to Your plans and yield to Your desires. Enable us to move in integrity, courage, and honesty. May our existence shine Your glory until the entire world is aware of the Lord's knowledge.

In the name of Jesus, Amen

Reflective Questions

1. Where have you seen injustice, corruption, or spiritual apathy in the Church or your community? What was your reaction, and what did you do?

_____

_____

_____

_____

Kingdom Challenge:

1. Fast and Pray Weekly: Set aside one day a week to fast and pray specifically for revival in your church, city, and nation.
2. Serve the Poor Intentionally: Like Daniel encouraged Nebuchadnezzar (Dan. 4:27), show mercy to the poor.
3. Confess personally and collectively the Church's sins in prayer and in trusted community. Ask God for cleansing and re-commissioning.

Final Chapter
God Has Spoken: Finish Your Race in Victory

1 Chronicles 29:11

"Yours, O Lord, is the greatness,

The power and the glory,

The victory and the majesty;

For all that is in heaven and in earth is Yours;

Yours is the kingdom, O Lord,

And You are exalted as head over all."

God has spoken—not vaguely, not silently, but clearly and consistently through His Word, His Spirit, and His Son. This book is a call to return to Him fully, obediently, and boldly. It is a cry for revival. A charge to proclaim His Kingdom. A declaration that God's Word is final.

What the Church Must Remember

- We are not simply members—we are **ambassadors of Christ**.

- Our call is not survival—it is **dominion, discipleship,**

and holiness.

- The Gospel is not optional—it is **our mandate**.

- Scripture is not outdated—it is **our lifeline and anchor**.

The Church must reclaim its authority and purity. We must stop compromising with darkness and start shining with divine light. The world is watching, and so is Heaven.

God's Desire for His People

Revelation 7:9

"A great multitude...from every nation, tribe, people, and language...standing before the Lamb."

Psalm 96:3

"Declare His glory among the nations, His marvelous deeds among all peoples."

God desires a Church without prejudice, compromise, or division—a people unified in truth, burning with love, and committed to justice. His Gospel is for **all**. His Kingdom is advancing, and we have a part to play.

The Final Call

The enemy has raged.
The Church has wrestled.

But God has spoken.

Let us rise and run our race with endurance.

Let us not grow weary.

Let us finish faithfully.

Like Jeremiah, may His Word burn in our bones.

Like Daniel, may we walk righteously in hostile lands.

Like Mary, may we magnify the Lord.

Like Jesus, may we say, "Not my will, but Yours be done."

Closing Declaration

We were born for this time.

We were called for this mission.

We were saved for this Kingdom.

Let every reader commit anew to knowing God's Word, obeying His commands, and loving people into His Kingdom.

God has spoken. Let His people say—Amen.

Reflect on These Questions:

1. What is God saying to me through this book?

2. What areas of my life need to come into alignment with His Word?

3. Am I walking in truth, love, and righteousness—or compromise?

4. How am I participating in the advancement of God's Kingdom?

5. Who in my life needs to encounter the love and salvation of Jesus?

Write Your Commitment:

Take a moment to write a prayer or declaration of faith in response to this journey. What will you do differently? What will you pursue more intentionally? What must you surrender?

Closing Prayer:

Lord, thank You for speaking.
Thank You for Your truth, Your Word, and Your Son.
Revive me. Refine me. Empower me.
Use me to glorify Your name and build Your Kingdom.
Make me bold in love, strong in truth, and faithful to the end.
I choose You—again and always.
Amen.

www.ingramcontent.com/pod-product-compliance
Lightning Source LLC
Chambersburg PA
CBHW051217120626
46547CB00013B/1388